The Three Little Pigs

Maggie Moore and Rob Hefferan

W

FRANKLIN WATTS

Once upon a time three little pigs
lived in a tiny house with their mother.
"It's time you left home," she grumbled.
"It's too crowded." So off they went.

Their mother waved them goodbye.
"Watch out for the big bad wolf," she
warned. "He will try to eat you."

"We're not afraid," laughed two little pigs. But the third little pig replied, "I'll be careful."

The first little pig met a man
carrying straw.

"That would make a cosy
house," he thought.

He quickly bundled the straw
together to make his house.

The second little pig met a man
carrying sticks.

"It's easy to make a house of
sticks," he thought.

He built his house very quickly.

The third little pig met a man
pulling a cart full of bricks.
"Bricks make a strong house,"
he said to himself and he carefully
built his house of bricks.

The wolf heard the pigs working and
crept up the hill. He saw the house
of straw.

"I can get an easy supper," he
grinned to himself.

But the first little pig saw the wolf coming.

"Little pig, little pig, let me in," whispered the wolf sweetly.

"Not by the hairs on my chinny chin chin," replied the little pig. "I will not let you in."

"Then I'll huff and I'll puff and I'll blow your house in," cried the wolf.

So he huffed and he puffed and he blew the house in. The first little pig rushed to the house of sticks.

The little pigs watched the wolf
running towards them.

"Little pig, little pig, let me in," growled the wolf.

"Not by the hairs on my chinny chin chin," squealed the second little pig. "I will not let you in."

"Then I'll huff and I'll puff and I'll blow your house in," shouted the wolf.

So he huffed and he puffed and he blew the house in. The little pigs scrambled down the hill to the house of bricks.

"Don't worry," said the third little pig as they watched the wolf galloping closer to them.

"Little pig, little pig, let me in," roared the wolf.

"Not by the hairs on my chinny chin chin," said the third little pig sternly. "I will not let you in."

"Then I'll huff and I'll puff and I'll blow your house in," bellowed the wolf.

So he huffed and he puffed until he had no breath left, but he could not blow the house in.

The three little pigs were safe!

The wolf was FURIOUS!

"I'll get those pigs," he muttered
and climbed onto the roof.

"You think you are so clever," he
shrieked, "but I'm coming to get you."

But the third little pig had put a pot of
boiling water under the chimney.

The wolf tumbled down the chimney into the pot. He wailed loudly and ran away with his tail between his legs and was never seen again.

The three little pigs lived happily ever after – and sometimes mother pig came to tea.

About the story

The Three Little Pigs story is included in Joseph Jacobs' *English Fairy Tales* in 1890, but it is thought to be a much older story than this. Joseph Jacobs was born in Australia in 1854, and came to England when he was 18 years old. He edited many fairy tale collections. He wanted English children to be able to read English fairy tales as well as those from France and Germany, which were already popular.

Be in the story!

Imagine you are Mother Pig coming for tea. What will you say to your three little pigs?

Now imagine you are the wolf telling your three little wolf cubs about your day.

First published in 2014 by
Franklin Watts
338 Euston Road
London
NW1 3BH

Franklin Watts Australia
Level 17/207 Kent Street
Sydney
NSW 2000

A CIP catalogue record for this book is available
from the British Library.

The artwork for this story first appeared in
Leapfrog: The Three Little Pigs

ISBN 978 1 4451 2823 8 (hbk)
ISBN 978 1 4451 2824 5 (pbk)
ISBN 978 1 4451 2826 9 (library ebook)
ISBN 978 1 4451 2825 2 (ebook)

Series Editor: Jackie Hamley
Series Advisor: Catherine Glavina
Series Designer: Cathryn Gilbert

Printed in China

Franklin Watts is a divison of
Hachette Children's Books,
an Hachette UK company.
www.hachette.co.uk